BIKER GEL...

CLEAN HUMOR

✝

BIKER JOKES
A Merry Heart Does Good Like A Medicine

A MERRY HEART DOES GOOD LIKE A MEDICINE

BIKER GEORGE CLEAN HUMOR

✝

BIKER JOKES

A Merry Heart Does Good Like A Medicine

VOLUME 1
AUTHOR: DANO JANOWSKI
FOREWORD BY: RICH VREELAND

More Biker George Books by Dano Janowski...
In The Wind With Biker George: Short Daily Ride Devotionals (Vol. 1)
In The Breeze With Biker George: Short Daily Ride Devotionals (Vol. 2)

Contents

ACKNOWLEDGMENTS	Page#5
COPYRIGHTS	Page#6
PREFACE & DISCLAIMER	Page#7
FOREWORD BY RICH VREELAND	Page#8
WHAT PEOPLE ARE SAYING	Page#11
CLEAN HUMOR + BIKER JOKES: **INDEX**	Page#15
CLEAN HUMOR + BIKER JOKES: **START**	Page#17
MERRY HEART SCRIPTURES	Page#91
HEALING SCRIPTURES	Page#95
EPILOGUE	Page#104
ABOUT THE AUTHOR	Page#105
VREELAND WINNER'S CIRCLE	Page#107

Acknowledgments

I wish I could personally thank everyone for their, support, inspiration, knowledge, & other help in creating this Biker George Book. I would never be able to list everyone that has been with me over the course of the years & I would hate to forget to mention someone. Therefore, I would like to publicly acknowledge my three foremost inspirations, my Lord Jesus Christ, my beautiful Wife, T, & my Dad.

Copyrights

(GW) Scripture taken from GOD'S WORD®, © 1995 God's Word to the Nations. Used by permission of Baker Publishing Group.

(KJV) Scripture taken from the King James Version which is in the Public Domain in the USA.

(NLT) Scripture quotations are taken from the Holy Bible, New Living Translation, Copyright ©1996, 2004, 2007, 2013, 2015 by Tyndale House Foundation. Used by permission of Tyndale House Publishers, Inc., Carol Stream, Illinois 60188. All rights reserved.

Copyright © 2018 by Dano Janowski
Cover Design Dano Janowski
All rights reserved

Amazon.com/author/dano
Facebook.com/BikerGeorgeBook

ISBN-13: 978-1729867525
ISBN-10: 1729867529

Preface & Disclaimer

Medical research has confirmed that Proverbs 17:22 really does good like a medicine & that a negative attitude can lead to health problems. Laughter can help with the healing process, & now days some hospitals even offer laughter therapy programs as a complementary treatment for patients! So, smile & laugh, & be healthy! Here are just a few things a merry heart can do for you:

- ✓ Improves cardiac health
- ✓ Trigger release of endorphins (body's natural painkillers)
- ✓ Ease digestion/soothe stomach aches
- ✓ Boosts T-cells (immediately helps you fight off sickness)
- ✓ Lower blood pressure
- ✓ Improve mental functions (i.e., alertness, memory, creativity)
- ✓ Improve overall attitude
- ✓ Reduce stress/tension
- ✓ Promote relaxation
- ✓ Improve sleep
- ✓ Enhance quality of life
- ✓ Strengthen social bonds & relationships
- ✓ Produce a general sense of well-being

Disclaimer: Please note some of these jokes are not politically correct or scripturally accurate they are to make you laugh. Some religious jokes may be controversial, so take it with a grain of salt & laugh! These are to help put a smile on your face & to give you a merry heart! Biker George would like to encourage you to smile & laugh often. A good way to get started is to read this book dedicated to giving you a Merry Heart via Clean Humor & Biker Jokes that you may not see anywhere else except here!

Try this book! It works! *Proverbs 17:22 (KJV) A merry heart doeth good like a medicine: but a broken spirit drieth the bones*

Foreword by Rich V.

Living in the world today brings stress & strain to us all. Learning to laugh & finding a reason to be cheerful makes a difference. Sometimes we need a little help to find the lighter side, but not Dano Janowski. He always has a smile on his face & a childlike joy! Dano has kept us on the narrow path with wisdom from Biker George. Dano's new work takes to a place of laughter. The Bible tells us the benefits of joy, real physical gain from a light heart. Walk with Dano in this healthy place, gain the benefit & bless others along the way. Enjoy the journey, ride hard & arrive safely at your Destination. Biker George would do no less.

Rich Vreeland, AMRA Harley Nitro Funny Bike Champion
& Co-Owner / Vreeland's Harley-Davidson Bloomsburg, PA

Rich's Testimony...
Life is one hard race. If anyone was least likely to win it, it was me. I never thought I'd be a winner.

My parents separated when I was 8. I went to live with my dad & rarely saw my mom. Dad worked long hours, & I spent most of my childhood alone. Alcoholism stole my family. I long to be loved. I wanted to be part of a real family.

At 13, I'd had enough. I hitch-hiked my way across the country from New Jersey to Colorado. I'd met a man back in Jersey, but he & his family moved to Colorado. He was a Godly Man, & he's taking me under his wing before. He was a mentor to me. I saw something in his life, & I wanted what he had. I lived with him & his family in Colorado for a year. He taught me a lot about our Heavenly Father & his unconditional love for us.
When I returned home, I attended church occasionally. But it wasn't long before God was in the background again. I pursued what I wanted. I'm married young & divorced just one year later. I

moved from job to job, looking for happiness. When my dad died in 1989, I never felt more alone.

My brother & I quit our jobs, hopped on our new Harley-Davidson & headed west. We rode around the country for a full month. I found myself back in Colorado with the same Godly Man. He encouraged my brother & I to follow our dream & open our own Harley-Davidson dealership. After 13 months of hard work, Vreeland's Harley-Davidson opened its doors in December 1990.

As the business grew, I had the opportunity to work on NASCAR's "Busch Grand National Series" race teams. I love the thrill of racing in the big leagues. I was away from home a lot. & even though I was able to go to Victory Lane 4 times with my team, there was still something missing. I didn't feel like a winner. When I started attending the Motor Racing Outreach Chapel Services, I made a choice. I finally moved God from the background to the front of my life. I surrendered my entire life to Jesus, was baptized, & started Living every area of my life for him. That is when I truly became a winner.

Win or lose at the track, I am victorious everyday over sins, problems, & the distractions of this world. Everyone can qualify for God's Team & you'll never find a better prize. Everyone can be a winner with God.

John 14: 1-4 tells about the security our Heavenly Father has for those who serve him. John 14: 1-4 (GW) "Don't be troubled. Believe in God, & believe in me. My Father's house has many rooms. If that were not true, would I have told you that I'm going to prepare a place for you? If I go to prepare a place for you, I will come again. Then I will bring you into my presence so that you will be where I am. You know the way to the place where I am going."

Staging is Important

★Acknowledge you're a sinner...

★Ask Jesus to forgive you...

★Invite Jesus into your heart...

★You're a new creation...

★Don't leave Earth without Jesus...

Philippians 3:12-14 (GW) It's not that I've already reached the goal or have already completed the course. But I run to win that which Jesus Christ has already won for me. Brothers & sisters, I can't consider myself a winner yet. This is what I do: I don't look back, I lengthen my stride, & I run straight toward the goal to win the prize that God's heavenly call offers in Christ Jesus.

Rich Vreeland, AMRA Harley Nitro Funny Bike Champion & Co-Owner / Vreeland's Harley-Davidson Bloomsburg, PA

What People Are Saying

I started reading the Biker George Clean Humor Biker Jokes Book & I couldn't put it down! When you can get an 84-year-old man to smile & chuckle you've accomplished a great feat!
~*Duane Janowski, Preacher, Teacher, & Dano's Dad & Mentor*

Great clean humor!!! Wholesome comedy safe for the whole family to enjoy!!! Enjoyed reading & had lots of good laughs!
~*Isaak Sawatzky, Canadian National President of the Heaven's Saints Motorcycle Ministry*

Good reading... You need to take some time & check this out.
~*Lil Wolf, Little Wolf Ministries*

There is a fine & purer laughter, & it belongs to the people of God. As brother Dano mentioned "A merry heart does good like a medicine" &, I might add, it's also a cure for the persimmon sucking sourness of many who are marching to Zion in Holy somber robes.
This book (& I read it all) made me laugh, chuckle, & even groan at a few. I always say a good eye roll is better than a laugh at times. I am happy to encourage you to read this book. Make no mistake this brother (AKA Biker George) can laugh freely because he has wept freely. He has a heart to bring people to know the Savior. Laughter is good & wholesome & it may loosen up a few of us old geezers. You ponder that...
~*Pastor Steve Nute, Biker Bible Institute*

Biker George is witty, funny & a lot of fun read. It is powerful to see great humor from a Christian Biker prospective!
~Pastor Mikey Seay, Biker Church USA

My first career was in broadcasting. We put together a morning show team made up of Tom, a musician, Dick, the announcer, & Harry. No one ever heard Harry. He was blamed for all of the mistakes & was the brunt of many jokes. His last name reveals his true identity—Figment.

Harry Figment has a brother, Biker George, who wants to help you live your life. The Bible says, "A merry heart doeth good like a medicine." Yes! From a scientific POV, laughter increases the feel-good endorphins in our brains. & this supports good health.

Author Dano is like a son to me. I do not remember when he did not have a brilliant & creative sense of clean humor! You will enjoy His "Biker George Clean Humor Biker Joke Book" Vol.1.
~Don Atkin, Author, Teacher, & Evangelist

Humor has its own special place on earth & in heaven! Thankfully, Brother Dano has learned that lesson & shares his special gift of humor-based wisdom with the rest of the Christian biker world. He does it almost daily on Facebook with his riding partner, "Biker George."

By now, most of us know that Abraham named his son Isaac. That's because God's prophecy made Abraham & Sarah laugh. & Isaac means "laughter" in Hebrew. Day by day, Christian bikers across America are discovering that there's more of Isaac in Brother Dano than any of us ever imagined. His latest book about "Biker George" settles that issue for sure!
Straight from "Isaac's Workshop," Brother Dano releases Biker

A MERRY HEART DOES GOOD LIKE A MEDICINE

George Clean Biker Jokes Volume 1. This is a must-read for everyone who has any part in the Christian biker world! While the humor in Clean Biker Jokes Volume 1 is quite good, the magic behind this book is genius! Two powerful words are behind each of the many jokes on its pages. Whether it was intended by Brother Dano or not, everything in this book says, "You're welcome."

When you read it, you will feel that you are not just a pretender. You belong with Brother Dano & the people around him. & you're welcome! When you share this book with a Christian biker friend who has strayed away from his faith, your friend will feel the message too — you're welcome. Come back! This is a book you can even give to your biker friends who are not Christians. Whether Brother Dano meant it or not, this is a wonderful tool that every Christian biker can give to another person & help them feel that maybe they could be welcome in the Kingdom of God too!

Humor works, folks! As Brother Dano rides through life with "Biker George," he shares his wonderful sense of humor & invites the rest of us to share the love of Jesus. This book is so much fun to read that we're ready to pull the spark plugs out of Brother Dano's bike so he has to return to "Isaac's Workshop" to start writing some more jokes & humorous stories!

Get this book, but don't keep it. Read it & then give it away. You can always get another one if you happen to run across someone else needing a clean joke & a good laugh! In Christ!
~Bro Franko, Christian Biker TV & a whole lot more

A MERRY HEART DOES GOOD LIKE A MEDICINE

Clean Humor + Biker Jokes
-=[INDEX]=-

- BIKER HITS SPARROW — PAGE#17
- BIKERS & DUCKS IN HEAVEN — PAGE#18
- BIKERS ON A SINKING SHIP — PAGE#19
- BIKERS & TRUCKER @ DINER — PAGE#20
- BIKER BELL RINGER — PAGE#21
- THE TEXAS & ISRAELI BIKER — PAGE#22
- BURLEY BIKER BRIBING A KID — PAGE#23
- BIKER @ COFFESSION SAYS NOTHING — PAGE#24
- BIKER @ CONFESSION CONFESSES — PAGE#25
- BIKER & 2 FOREIGNERS ON A FLIGHT — PAGE#26
- BIKER CHICK & EX IN HEAVEN — PAGE#27
- RABBI & PRIEST IN ACCIDENT — PAGE#28
- BIKER GIVES PASTOR DIRECTIONS — PAGE#29
- BIKER BUYS POSTAL STAMPS — PAGE#30
- TAKE HARLEY TO HEAVEN — PAGE#31
- BIKER & OLD LADY GET PULLED — PAGE#32
- IS JESUS WHITE OR BLACK? — PAGE#33
- THREE HIGH TECH BIKERS — PAGE#34
- BIKER IN JAIL & HIS DAD'S FARM — PAGE#35
- BIKER "WANNA BE" APPEARS B4 ST. PETE — PAGE#36
- BIKER SKIPS CHURCH & MEETS A BEAR — PAGE#37
- BIKE PUTTERING AT 22 MPH — PAGE#38
- TWO PRIESTS RIDING A HARLEY — PAGE#39
- BIKER HELPS LADY LOCKED OUT OF CAR — PAGE#40
- BIKER HIT BY PASTOR'S CAR — PAGE#41
- BURGLER CAUGHT IN THE ACT — PAGE#42
- ASK ABOUT BIG FISH WHEN IN HEAVEN — PAGE#43
- BIKER CALMS DOWN LOUD KID — PAGE#44
- SEMI CAUSES MOTORCYCLE WRECK — PAGE#45
- LOVELY HEAVEN TIL BIKER PROBLEMS — PAGE#46
- BIKER VISITS MENTAL HOSPITAL — PAGE#47
- BIKER'S REWARD IN HEAVEN — PAGE#48
- DRINKING DRIVER PULLED — PAGE#49
- NO RIGHT TURN ON RED — PAGE#50
- NATIVE AMERICAN WEATHER — PAGE#51
- PERFECT COUPLE & SANTA — PAGE#52

- THE WALLS OF JERICHO — PAGE#53
- BIKER CHICK & FINE APPLES — PAGE#54
- A RUB ARRIVES IN HEAVEN — PAGE#55
- NEW KIND OF MOTORCYCLE — PAGE#56
- BIKER CHICK PLASTIC SURGERY — PAGE#57
- BIKER GETS A GOLDEN STAFF — PAGE#58
- 3 QUESTIONS IN HEAVEN — PAGE#59
- LONG WHITE HAIR & BEARD — PAGE#60
- HARLEY PULLED AT 120 MPH — PAGE#61
- WATER IN THE CARBURETOR — PAGE#62
- YUPPIE BIKER RUNS STOP SIGN — PAGE#63
- THE FASTEST MOTORCYCLE — PAGE#64
- A BRIDGE TO HAWAII — PAGE#65
- DOBERMAN VS POODLE PUPPY — PAGE#66
- BIKER & MEXICAN BORDER — PAGE#67
- BE QUIET PASSING ROOM #7 — PAGE#68
- ATHEIST & LOCH NESS MONSTER — PAGE#69
- PRAY FOR BUBBA'S HEARING — PAGE#70
- JESUS IS GONNA GET YOU — PAGE#71
- ANYONE KNOW HOW TO PRAY? — PAGE#72
- MEAN DOG & LITTLE UGLY DOG — PAGE#73
- BIKER DRANK BRAKE FLUID — PAGE#74
- BIKER CHICK MOPPED FLOOR — PAGE#75
- BAPTIZED IN CHURCH POND — PAGE#76
- BIKER GEORGE PASSES GAS — PAGE#77
- BIKER PAINTS FOR GAS MONEY — PAGE#78
- FATHER CAUGHT SPEEDING — PAGE#79
- TELL A DUMB BLONDE JOKE? — PAGE#80
- BIKER GEORGE HORSE RIDING — PAGE#81
- LITTLE GUY & THE BIG BIKER — PAGE#82
- TEXAS BIKER & GREAT BEYOND — PAGE#83
- LOT'S WIFE TURNED INTO SALT — PAGE#84
- CHILD SAVED FROM MEAN DOG — PAGE#85
- LITTLE LIP PRINTS ON MIRROR — PAGE#86
- BIKER & THE TALKING FROG — PAGE#87
- BIKER TEACHES SELF-ESTEEM — PAGE#88
- BIKER NIGHT B4 CHRISTMAS — PAGE#89

Clean Humor + Biker Jokes
-=[Start Here]=-

BIKER HITS SPARROW

A biker is riding along a country lane, when a sparrow flies up in front of him. The biker can't do anything & hits the sparrow. As he looks in his rear-view mirror, he sees the sparrow lying in the road.

Being the tender-hearted guy, he is, he stops, picks up the sparrow & takes it home & puts it in a cage, while it's still in a coma.

When sparrow wakes up the following morning, he looks through the bars of the cage & says, "OH NO! I must have killed the biker!"

BIKERS & DUCKS IN HEAVEN

Three bikers die in an accident & arrive at the pearly gates of Heaven. St. Peter greets them & tells them "Whatever you do, don't step on a duck!" Well, the bikers thought that sounded very odd, but when they enter Heaven, they look around & there are ducks EVERYWHERE!

The 1st biker was talking to the 2nd and, not paying attention, stepped on a duck. St. Peter appears at his side with a pair of handcuffs & a very ugly woman. "Now that you have stepped on a duck, you shall be chained to this hideous looking woman for the rest of your days here."

A few weeks later, the 2nd biker suffers the same fate.

Now the 3rd biker is determined to not step on a duck. Years go by, & he's yet to step on a duck. All of sudden St. Peter appears with the most beautiful woman he'd ever laid eyes on & handcuffs them together & walks away without saying a word.

The biker asks the beautiful lady "Whatever have I done to deserve this?" "I don't know about you, but I stepped on a duck" says the woman.

BIKERS ON A SINKING SHIP

A Honda rider went on vacation via one of those Harley-Davidson Cruise Ship deals. Half way through the voyage, the ship sank & he ended up in a three-man lifeboat with two Harley riders & the ship's captain for a total of 4 people.

The captain announced that someone would have to get out. "We'll do it right though," he said. "The three of you will be given a fair test & the loser will jump out." Everyone agreed, so the captain turned to one of the Harley riders & asked, "What was the largest ocean liner to sink in the past century?"

"The Titanic."

"Right," said the captain. Turning to the other Harley rider, he asked, "How many were on the Titanic?"

"2463"

"That's correct," the captain stated.

Fixing a hard eye on the Honda rider, he then said, "Name 'em."

BIKERS & TRUCKER @ DINER

A young truck driver pulls into a diner & orders a hamburger, French fries, & coke. While sitting at the counter, a group of bikers pulled in, started acting rowdy, knocked his coke over, grabbed his burger & fries & ate them.

Then they threatened to beat him up if he says anything to anyone about them.

The trucker quietly gets up, pays for his meal, walks out & drives off.

One of the bikers said to the waitress: "My, that trucker wasn't much of a man, was he?"

The waitress replied back with "No, & he's not much of a driver either, he just ran over six motorcycles!"

BIKER BELL RINGER

Once upon a time after Quasimodo's death, the Bishop of Notre Dame sent word out that they needed a new bell ringer. The bishop decided to conduct interviews personally & went up into the belfry to begin the screening process. After observing several applicants demonstrate their bell ringing skills, he decided to call it a day.

Just then a lone, armless man (who lost both of his arms in a motorcycle accident) approached him & announced that he's there to apply for the bell ringer's job. Bishop Thomas was incredulous. "But you have no arms sir." "No matter," said the man, "observe!" He then began striking the bells with his face, producing a beautiful melody. The bishop listened in astonishment, convinced that he had finally found a suitable replacement for Quasimodo.

A minute later it was officially time for the ringing of the bell, so the armless man ran forward to strike the bell but tripped & plunged head first out of the belfry to his death in the street below!

The stunned bishop ran down the winding stairway & when he reached the street there was a large crowd gathered around the fallen figure. They all were drawn by the beautiful music they had heard only moments before.

As they silently parted to let the bishop through, one of them asked, "Bishop, who was this man?" "I don't know his name," the bishop sadly replied, "but his face sure rings a bell."

TEXAS & ISRAELI BIKER

A Texas rancher was visiting a farm in Israel. The proud Israeli showed him around & pointed out his many crops on a small piece of property.

The Texan was surprised on how little the land was. "Is this all your land?" he asked with a demeaning tone.

"Yes," the Israeli said proudly. "This is all mine!"

"Well, son," said the Texan, "back home I'd get on my motorcycle before the sun come up & I'd ride & ride till the sun set, & I'd only be halfway across my land!"

"Oh yes," replied the Israeli farmer laughing at the Texan, "I used to have a motorcycle like that."

BURLEY BIKER BRIBING KID

A ten-year-old boy was walking down the street when a big old burly man on a black Harley, pulls up beside him & asks, "Hey kid, wanna go for a ride?"

"No!" said the boy & he kept on walking.

The biker pulls up to him again & says; "Hey kid, I'll give you $10 if you hop on the back"

"NO!" said the boy & proceeded down the street a little quicker.

The big old biker pulls up to the boy again & says, "Ok kid, I'll give you $20 & a BIG bag of candy if you hop on the back for a ride."

At this point the boy turns around to him & screams angrily, "Look Dad, YOU bought the motorcycle, so YOU ride it!!"

BIKER @ COFFESSION BOX SAYS NOTHING AT FIRST

A Harley pulls up to a Catholic Church & an old drunken tattooed biker staggers through the doorway & sits down in a confession box & says nothing.

The bewildered priest coughs to attract his attention, but still the old biker says nothing. The priest then knocks loudly on the wall in a final attempt to get him to speak & start his confession.

Finally, the drunken biker replies: "No use knockin' bro, there's no paper in this one either."

BIKER AT CONFESSIONAL STARTS TO CONFESS TO PRIEST

A Biker pulls up to a Catholic Church, gets off his motorcycle, enters the church, & heads toward the confessional.

He sits down in the confession box where much to his surprise he finds a full mini bar & a wide selection of cigars.

Then the priest comes in & the biker starts his confession "Father forgive me. My last confession was a very long time ago & since then these confession boxes are more inviting than they used to be.

The priest replies "You're on my side of the box, get out of there!"

BIKER & TWO FOREIGNERS ON A FLIGHT TOGETHER

Two Foreigners boarded a flight out of London. One took a window seat & the other sat next to him in the middle seat.

Just before takeoff, an American Biker sat down in the aisle seat by the two Foreigners.

After takeoff, the Biker kicked his boots off, wiggled his toes & was settling in when the Foreigner in the window seat said, "I need to get up & get a coke."

"Don't get up," said the Biker, "I'm in the aisle seat; I'll get it for you."

As soon as he left, one of the Foreigners picked up the Biker's boot & spat in it.

When he returned with the coke, the other Foreigner said, "That looks good, I'd really like one, too." Again, the Biker obligingly went to fetch it. While he was gone the other Foreigner picked up his other boot & spat in it. When the Biker returned, they all sat back & enjoyed the flight. As the plane was landing, the Biker slipped his feet into his boots & knew immediately what had happened.

"Why does it have to be this way?" he asked. "How long must this go on? This fighting between our nations? This hatred? This animosity? This spitting in boots & peeing in cokes?"

BIKER CHICK & EX IN HEAVEN

A biker chick dies & arrives at the Pearly Gates. Saint Peter tells her "You can't come in unless you spell a word".

"What word?" the woman asked.

"Any word" says Peter.

So, she spells "L-O-V-E" & Peter says "Welcome to Heaven!" Then Peter asks her if she would take his place for a little while. He instructs her to follow the same procedure in case anyone else comes up.

In just a few minutes she sees her ex-husband coming up. She says "What are you doing here?"

He says "I just had a heart attack. Did I really make it to Heaven?"

She says, "Not yet, you have to correctly spell a word."

"Which word?" her ex asks.

After a short pause she responds, "Czechoslovakia."

RABBI & PRIEST IN ACCIDENT

A Rabbi & a Priest are riding their motorcycles one day and, by a freak accident, have a head-on collision with each other. Both bikes are totaled, but they are both OK.

The rabbi sees the priest's collar & says, "So you're a priest. I'm a rabbi. Our bikes are totaled yet we are safe & not hurt. This must be a sign from God!" Pointing to the sky, he continues, "God must have meant that we should meet & share our lives in peace & friendship for the rest of our days on earth." The priest replies, "I agree with you completely. This must surely be a sign from God!" The rabbi is looking at his bike & exclaims, "Look at this! Here's another miracle! My motorcycle is completely demolished, but this bottle of Mogen David wine did not break. Surely, God wants us to drink this wine & to celebrate our good fortune." The priest nods in agreement.

The rabbi hands the bottle to the priest, who drinks half the bottle & hands the bottle back to the rabbi. The rabbi takes the bottle & immediately puts the cap on, then hands it back to the priest.

The priest, baffled, asks, "Aren't you having any, Rabbi?" The rabbi replies, "Nah... I think I'll wait for the police."

BIKER GIVES A PASTOR DIRECTIONS TO POST OFFICE

A guy in a car pulls up to a group of bikers. He rolls down his window & asks the leader if he could give him directions to the Post Office.

The biker tells him take a left at the next light & it's about a mile up on the right with a big sign that says US Post Office.

The man in the car tells him thank you & says, by the way, I'm the new Pastor in town. If would like to come to my church on Sunday I'll give you directions to get to heaven.

The biker looks at him & says No thanks, you can't even get to the Post Office!

BIKER BUYS POSTAL STAMPS

A Christian Biker went to Post Office to get some stamps.

The clerk behind the counter asks him "What denominations"?

The biker yells out, "Has it come to this???!!!

OK...

Then let me have...
10 Charismatic,
10 Baptist,
10 Methodist,
10 Lutheran,
& 10 Catholic!"

BIKER ON HIS DEATH BED WANTS TO TAKE HIS HARLEY TO HEAVEN

An old biker is laying on his death bed & he wants to take his Harley with him when dies, so that he can ride it in heaven on those streets of gold.

So, he tells his old lady to have his bike put on the roof, telling her that he would grab it on the way to heaven.

The biker passes away that evening.

The next day his old lady & club members see that his Harley is still on the roof.

His wife shouts out, "I knew we should have put his stuff in the basement!"

BIKER & HIS OLD LADY GET PULLED OVER BY A COP

A motorcycle is pulled over by a cop & the following conversation takes place...

Biker: What's the problem officer?

Cop: You were going at least 75 in a 55 zone.

Biker: No sir, I was going 65.

Old Lady on passenger seat: Oh Bubba...You were going 80.

Cop: I'm also gonna give you a ticket for the broke tail light.

Biker: Broke tail light? I didn't know about a broken light!

Old Lady: Oh Bubba, you've known about that tail light for weeks. (Man gives Old Lady a dirty look.)

Cop: I'm also going to give you a citation for not using your turn signal when you pulled over.

Biker: Oh, I just turned them off when you were walking up!

Old Lady: Oh Bubba, your turn signals never worked.

Biker: Shut your mouth, woman!

Cop: Ma'am, does your husband always talk to you this way?

Old Lady: No, only when he's drunk.

TWO BIKERS ASK "IS JESUS IS WHITE OR BLACK?"

Once upon a time there was two Christian bikers that have been riding together for several years.

They always seem to see eye to eye on most all spiritual matters except for one. Roadkill insisted that Jesus was white & Tyrone was sure Jesus is black.

As fate seem to have it, they both died the same day & with anticipation they strolled up to the pearly gates together & asked St Peter to tell them if Jesus was white or black.

Just then, Jesus comes be-bopping around the corner & greets them saying "Buenos dias amigos"!

THREE HIGH TECH BIKERS

Three Bikers, a Sport Bike Rider, BMW Rider & Harley Biker were sitting in a sauna when a beeping sound started.

The Sport bike Rider pressed his forearm & the beeping stopped. The others looked at him questioningly. "That was my pager, "he said, "I have a pager microchip under the skin of my arm."

A few minutes later a phone rang. The BMW Rider lifted his palm to his ear. When he finished, he explained, "That was my cell phone. I had a small proto-type implanted in my hand."

The Harley Rider felt really low tech. Not to be outdone, he decided he had to do something just as impressive. He stepped out of the sauna & went to the bathroom. He returned with a piece of toilet paper hanging from his butt. The others raised their eyebrows & stared at him.

The Harley Rider finally declared... "Well, will you look at that, I'm getting a fax!"

CAN A BIKER IN JAIL HELP HIS DAD ON THE FARM?

An old farmer is trying to keep his farm going until his biker son can get out of jail to help him.

The farmer emails him in jail wishing he could help him plant the potato crop.

The biker emails his father back: "Dad, don't go near the field. That's where the guns are buried."

But, because he is in jail & all of the inmate emails are censored, the sheriff & his deputies catch this & they all run out to the farm & dig up the entire field looking for guns. After two full days of digging, they don't find one single weapon.

The biker writes back to his dad, "Hope that the sheriff & his deputies helped you out some...that's the best I can do from inside here!"

BIKER "WANNA BE" APPEARS BEFORE ST. PETER AT THE PEARLY GATES

A biker "wanna be" appeared before St. Peter at the Pearly Gates.

"Have you ever done anything of particular merit?" St. Peter asked.

"Well, I can think of one thing," the man offered. "Once, on a trip to the Black Hills of South Dakota, I came upon a gang of mean bikers who were threatening a young woman. I directed them to leave her alone, but they wouldn't listen." "So, I approached the largest & most heavily tattooed biker & smacked him in the face, kicked his bike over, ripped out his nose ring, & threw it on the ground. I yelled, "Now, back off, or I'll kick the heck out of all of you!"

St. Peter was very impressed & asked. "When did this happen?"

"Just a couple of minutes ago."

BIKER SKIPS CHURCH, GOES ON A RIDE & THEN MEETS A BEAR

It was a beautiful sun shiny day when a biker decided to skip church this one Sunday to go riding in the mountains. As he was going around one of the sweeping curves, he saw a huge grizzly bear in the middle of the road.

He swerved to miss it & just barley grazed it. The bike lost traction because of loose gravel on the side of the road & then went over the edge & began tumbling down the side of the mountain with the angry bear chasing him.

Finally, the bike came to a rest after it & the biker was slammed up against a giant tree, breaking both of his legs.

As the bear closed in, the biker cried out in desperation, "Lord, I'm sorry for what I have done. Please forgive me & save me! Lord, please make that bear a Christian."

Suddenly, the clouds parted & a beam of light shown down on the bear.

The bear skidded to a halt at the biker's feet, fell to its knees, clasped its paws together & said, "God, bless this food which I am about to receive."

BIKE PUTTERING AT 22 MPH

A State Patrol sees a motorcycle puttering down the middle of the interstate at 22 MPH & he says to himself, "This is just as dangerous as speeders!" He turns on his lights & pulls the bike over.

Approaching, he notices it is an elderly gentleman with a wide eyed, white as a ghost biker chick on the back.

The old biker obviously confused, says to the officer, "I don't understand, I was doing the speed limit! What seems to be the problem?"

The officer replies, "You weren't speeding, but you should know that driving way slower than the speed limit can also be a danger to you & other drivers."

I was doing the speed limit exactly... Twenty-Two miles an hour!" the old biker says a bit cocky.

The State Patrol, trying to contain a chuckle explains to him that "22" was the route number, not the speed limit.

A bit embarrassed, the old man grinned & thanked the officer for pointing out the error, & started to ride off.

The officer says "Hold on... Before I let ya go, I have to ask... Is your passenger OK? Your old lady seems awfully shaken & she hasn't muttered a single peep this whole time."

"Oh, she'll be alright in a minute officer. We just got off Route 119."

TWO PRIESTS ON A HARLEY

Two priests were speeding down the highway on a Harley. They were stopped by a cop who said, "What do y'all think you're doing? You were going mighty fast there, Father."

The priest says, "We were just taking the bike for a test run."

The officer shakes his head. "I'm probably gonna have to give you a ticket cause riding like that just ain't safe. What if you had an accident?"

The priests say, "Don't worry, my son. Jesus is with us."

The policeman says, "In that case, I have to book you! Three people are not allowed to ride on one motorcycle!"

BIKER HELPS A LADY THAT IS LOCKED OUT OF HER CAR

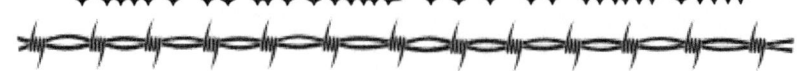

It's a dark scary night on the bad side of town where a pretty young Christian lady locks her cell phone & keys in her car.

Shaken with the situation, she bows her head & asks God to please send her some help. Within a few minutes a grungy mean looking biker on a loud rat bike pulls up. The woman thinking, she is about to be brutally murdered, mutters under her breath "Thanks God, but I really didn't want to die this way".

The heavily tattooed & pierced biker jumps off his bike & approaches her, asking if he could help. She says with a nervous stutter, "Yes, I've locked my keys in my car. Can you help me?"

He picks up an old rusty hanger from the gutter, bends it, raises it above his head & plunges it down inside the window towards the door lock & in a few seconds he opens the car door. She suddenly hugs the nasty looking biker & through her tears she says, "Thank You So Much! You are a very nice man."

The biker replies, "Lady, I'm not a nice man. I just got out of prison for car theft & have only been out for about an hour."

The woman hugs him again & with sobbing tears cried out loud, "Oh, Thank you God! You even sent me a Professional!"

BIKER HIT BY PASTOR'S CAR

The Reverend Malcolm Livingston was not the best of drivers.

One Sunday he was driving home from church when he had a minor bump up with a motorcyclist. The rider was knocked off his motorcycle, but he & his bike were OK.

The pastor stopped his car, apologized repeatedly, & gave the biker his calling card saying that if he could ever be of help to give him a call anytime.

As the biker rode home, he looked down at the card which said, "The Reverend Malcolm Livingston is sorry he missed you today."

BURGLER CAUGHT ROBBING HOUSE

An elderly woman had just returned to her home from church service when she was startled by an intruder. She catches a man in the act of robbing her home & yells, "Stop! Acts 2:38!" [Turn from your sin]

The burglar stopped dead in his tracks. Then the woman calmly called the police & explained what she had done.

As the officer cuffed the man to take him in, he asked the burglar, "Why did you just stand there? All the old lady did was yell a scripture at you."

"Scripture?" replies the burglar, "She said she had an axe & two 38s!"

BIKER TO ASK ABOUT BIG FISH WHEN HE GETS TO HEAVEN

A Christian Biker on a flight was reading his Bible, when another biker sitting next to him asked if he really believed all the things in his Bible, especially that stuff about the guy in the belly of the whale. Christian Biker replied, "Of course I do because God said so." "I'll ask Jonah about his days in the belly of the big fish when I get to heaven."

The other biker, wanting to argue, replied "What if he ain't up there in heaven?"

The Christian Biker replied "Then you can ask him."

BIKER CALMS A LOUD KID

A crowded flight is about to take off when the peace is shattered by a 5-year-old boy who decides to throw a wild temper tantrum. His embarrassed mom tries hard to calm him down but nothing works. The boy continues to scream & have a fit while thrashing about & kicking the seats around him.

Suddenly, from the rear of the plane, an old biker wearing his colors is seen slowly walking forward up the aisle. He asks the mom if he can help & leans down and, motioning toward his chest, whispers something into the boy's ear.

Instantly, the boy calms down, gently takes his mother's hand, & quietly fastens his seat belt. All the other passengers burst into spontaneous applause.

As the biker slowly makes his way back to his seat, one of the flight attendants says "Excuse me, sir, but what magic words did you use on that little boy?"

The old biker smiles serenely & gently confides, "I showed him my HOG patch, HOG pins, plus all the different rally pins, & explained that they entitle me to throw one passenger out the plane door on any flight I choose."

BIG SEMI-TRUCK CAUSES MOTORCYCLE TO WRECK

Several weeks after a semi-truck caused Biker Joe to have a wreck, he went to court suing for medical expenses. The trucking company lawyer asked him "How can you sue when at the scene of the accident, you said 'I'm fine'?"

Well... says Biker Joe as he starts his story... I was pulling my custom doggy trailer behind the Harley where my buddy Rocky the Rottweiler rides with me. Me & Rocky loved the ride until a semi-truck ditched us off the road. I was thrown into a big ditch & Rocky landed about 100 feet away. I was hurting bad & sure both my arms & legs were broken because of the bad pain. I heard Rocky whimpering & knew Rocky's injuries had to be bad, too. Few minutes after the accident a Highway Patrolman arrived. He came up on Rocky first. Poor Rocky looked really bad & was lying in a big pool of blood. After the officer looked at Rocky, he shot him between the eyes.

Then the Patrolman came up the road with his gun in hand to me "Your dog was in bad shape I had to shoot him. How are you feeling?" I'm had to reply I'M FINE! What would you say!?

BEAUTIFUL DAY IN HEAVEN TIL BIKERS CAUSING PROBLEMS

It was a beautiful day in heaven when St. Pete came to the Lord & said, "I gotta talk to you. We got some Bikers up here who are causing problems. They're swinging on the pearly gates, they're wearing T-shirts instead of robes; there's BBQ sauce & salsa everywhere including their T-shirts; their dogs are riding in the chariots & chasing the sheep; they're wearing Doo Rags & Baseball Caps instead of their halos. They refuse to keep the stairway to heaven clean, & their boots are leaving black marks on the streets of gold. There are sun flower seeds & hot wing bones all over the place. They refuse to walk & insist on riding their Harleys instead."

The Lord said, "Bikers are Bikers, St. Pete... Heaven is Home to all my children... If you want to hear some real problems, call the Devil."

The Devil answered the phone, "Hello... hold on a minute." The Devil returned to the phone, "OK, I'm back. What can I do for you?" St. Pete replied, "I just wanna know what kinda biker problems you're having down there." The Devil says, "Hold on again. I need to check on something." After about 5 minutes the Devil returned to the phone & said, "I'm back. Now what was the question?" St. Pete said, "What kinda problems are you having down there?" The Devil said, "I don't believe this ... Hold on." This time the Devil was gone 15 minutes. The Devil returned & said, "I'm sorry St. Pete, can't talk right now. Those Bikers put out the fire & are trying to install air conditioning!"

VISITING MENTAL HOSPITAL

Biker George visited a mental hospital & asked the director how they determine whether or not a patient is unstable & whether or not they need to be committed.

"We fill a bathtub, give them a spoon, a cup & a bucket, & ask the patient to empty the bathtub." says the director.

Oh, I see," said the Biker George. "A normal person would use the bucket because it is bigger than the spoon or the teacup."

"No," said the director, "a normal person would pull out the plug. Do you want the bed near the window?"

BIKER'S REWARD IN HEAVEN

A Christian Biker dies & goes to Heaven.

Saint Pete tells him "For your righteousness you'll be given something to ride on the streets of gold" Saint Pete led him past several really nice motorcycles, stopping at a moped.

The old biker gets on the moped & rides around sadly for weeks.

Finally, Saint Pete sees him smiling down the road. He asks "Why are you happy? You have been looking really sad for weeks!"

The biker replies "I just saw the president from a GMC on roller skates!"

DRINKING DRIVER PULLED

Two guys get pulled over while drinking & driving. The driver tells his friend, "Peel the labels off these beer bottles, & we'll each stick one on our forehead. Now, shove all of the bottles under the front seat & let me do all the talking."

The cop walks up & shines his flashlight into the car. "Have you been drinking?" he asks.

"No, sir," the drunk answers. "We haven't had a thing to drink tonight."

"Then what on earth are those beer labels doing on your foreheads?"

"We're both alcoholics," says the drunk. "We're on the patch."

BIKER TURNS WHEN SIGN SAYS NO RIGHT TURN ON RED

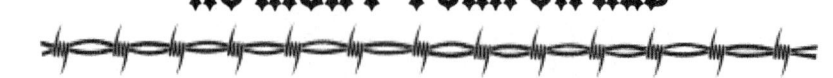

Biker George & Angel were a little late getting started out one morning to get to a benefit ride. They decided they would ride as fast as they can, but not too fast.

Being in a hurry, they made a right turn at a red light where it said "NO RIGHT TURN ON RED" to save some time.

Then it hit him & George said... "Oh no... I just made an illegal turn back there!"

Angel says... "Honey, I'm sure it's OK... The cop car right behind us just did the same thing too."

NATIVE AMERICAN WEATHER

Flying Eagle was a Native American Biker that was recently voted in as Chief of his tribe. At their tribal meeting he was asked if this was going to be a cold winter. He really wasn't sure, but replied that the winter was going to be really cold & they should gather a lot of fire wood to be prepared.

He was asked this question often by the village as winter was fast approaching & each time he told them it was going to be really cold, to gather more wood.

Each time Flying Eagle checked with the local weatherman to confirm.

The last time he called the weatherman, the weatherman replied "I am positive it's going to be a very cold winter because the Indians are collecting wood like crazy!"

PERFECT COUPLE & SANTA

Once upon a time, a perfect man & a perfect woman met (both were bikers, of course). After a perfect courtship, they had a perfect wedding. Their life was, of course "perfect."

One snowy, stormy Christmas Eve, this perfect couple was driving along in their perfect 4-wheel drive truck when they noticed someone stranded on the side of the road.

There stood Santa Claus with a huge bundle of toys. The perfect couple loaded Santa & his toys into their vehicle & off they went to save Christmas.

The driving conditions got really bad & the perfect couple with Santa Claus got in an accident. Only one of them survived the accident.

Who was the survivor?

The perfect woman survived. She's the only one who really existed in the first place. Everyone knows there is no Santa Claus & there is no such thing as a perfect man!

So, if there is no perfect man & no Santa Claus, the perfect woman must have been driving. This could explain why there was an accident, too.

THE WALLS OF JERICHO

Sunday school teacher asks little Johnny during Bible class who broke down the walls of Jericho.

Little Johnny replies that he does not know, but it wasn't him.

The teacher, couldn't believe the lack of basic Bible knowledge & goes to the head deacon to tell him of the whole incident. The deacon replies that he knows little Johnny as well as his whole family very well & can vouch for them, if little Johnny said that he did not do it, he as head deacon is satisfied that it is the truth.

Even more appalled the teacher goes to the regional Head of Church Affairs & relates the whole story.

After listening he replies: "I cannot see why you are making such a big issue out of this; we will get three quotations & fix the darn wall!"

BIKER CHICK & FINE APPLES

A pretty biker chick went to the farmer's market to buy some apples.

She asked the farmer "How much are these fine apples?"

"Only one kiss per apple" replied the wise guy.

"That's fine," replied the girl. "I'll take a dozen of them."

With expectation & anticipation written all over his face, the farmer hurriedly bagged up the apples & held them out teasingly.

The girl snapped up the bag & pointed to a little old man standing beside her. "Grandpa will pay the bill," she smiled.

A RUB ARRIVES IN HEAVEN

A Rich Urban Biker (AKA: RUB) died & arrived to Heaven.

Saint Peter asks him "What have you done to merit entrance into Heaven?"

The RUB thought a moment, then said, "A week ago, I gave a quarter to a homeless person on the street."

Saint Pete asked Gabriel to check this out in the records, & after a moment Gabriel affirmed that this was true.

Saint Peter said, "Well, that's fine, but it's not really quite enough to get you into Heaven." The RUB said, "Wait Wait! Three years ago, I also gave another homeless person a quarter." Saint Peter nodded to Gabriel, who after a moment nodded back, affirming this, too, had been verified.

Saint Peter then whispered to Gabriel, "Well, what do you suggest we do with this fellow?"

Gabriel gave the RUB a sidelong glance, then said to Saint Peter, "Let's give him back his 50 cents & tell him to go to Hell."

NEW KIND OF MOTORCYCLE

Two guys sat down for lunch at the local bike shop.

"Hey, whatever happened to Pete in the parts dept?" one asked.

"He got this harebrained notion he was gonna build a new kind of motorcycle," his co-worker replied.

"How was he going to do it?" "Well...He took a motor from a Harley, wheels from a Victory, seat from an Indian, and, well, you get the idea."

"So, what did he end up with?" "10 years to life."

BIKER CHICK GETS PLASTIC SURGERY

A biker chick had a heart attack & was taken to the hospital.

Her near-death experience landed her in the presence of God & she asked "Is my time up?" God said, "No, you have another 43 years, 2 months, & 8 days to live."

She decided to stay in the hospital & have a facelift, liposuction, & a tummy tuck. She even died her hair. Since she had so much more time to live, she figured she might as well make the most of it.

Three weeks later she was recovered from the plastic surgery & was riding home on her scoot when she was killed instantly by a speeding tractor trailer!

Arriving in front of God, she yelled, "I thought you said I had another 40+ years!? Why didn't you save me from being hit by that speeding tractor trailer!?"

God replied, "I didn't recognize you!"

BIKER GETS A GOLDEN STAFF

Biker Joe's last job before he passed away was a cab driver.

Well, he gets to the pearly gates & St. Pete greets him, finds his name in the Big Book, gives him a golden staff, a beautiful white silk robe & tells him to proceed into Heaven.

Next in line is an old preacher. St. Peter looks him up in the Book, & says, "OK, we'll let you in... Grab that cheap robe & wooden walking stick."

The preacher is shocked & replies, "A cabbie gets gold & silk & this is all I get? I'll let you know that I am a man of the cloth & should surely rate higher than a cab driver!"

St. Peter responds, "Up here, we are interested in results. When you preached, people slept. When Biker Joe drove his taxi, people prayed!"

3 QUESTIONS IN HEAVEN

Biker Joe died & went to heaven. When he got to the Pearly Gates, Saint Peter told him he must answer three questions first. 1. Name two days of the week that begin with "T". 2. How many seconds are in a year? 3. What's God's first name?

Biker Joe thought for a few minutes & answered "1. The two days of the week that begin with "T" are Today & Tomorrow... 2. There are 12 seconds in a year... 3. God has two first names & they are ANDY & HOWARD."

Saint Pete said, "OK I'll buy Today & Tomorrow, even though it's not the answer I wanted. How did you get 12 seconds in a year & why do you think God's 1st name is ANDY or HOWARD?"

Biker Joe: "Well, January 2nd, February 2nd, March 2nd, etc."

"OK, I give" said Saint Peter, "but what about God's first name stuff?"

Biker Joe said "Well, from the song... ANDY walks with me, ANDY talks with me; ANDY tells me I am his own... & the prayer... Our Father who art in Heaven, HOWARD be thy name..." Saint Peter then said, welcome to heaven!

LONG WHITE HAIR & BEARD

One day, Jesus was walking by the Pearly Gates, when St. Peter asked him to watch the gates for a few minutes.

Jesus agreed & in a few minutes he saw an old, old man approach with long white hair & beard. "How did you spend your life on earth my son?" asked Jesus.

"I was a simple carpenter for sixty years" replied the old man.

"And what do you hope to find here in heaven" asked Jesus.

"I hope to find my son" said the man.

"Well there are millions upon millions of people here, how will you find him?"

"I'll recognize him by the nail holes in his hands & feet," states the old man.

Jesus does a double take, thinks for a moment & says, "Father???"

The old man looks at Jesus & says, "Pinocchio?"

HARLEY PULLED AT 120 MPH

A guy bought a new Harley & got onto the interstate to see how fast it would go. As he got up to 80mph he suddenly saw a flashing blue light behind him. He sped up to 120 but the highway patrol was still on his tail.

He finally pulled over & the cop came up to him, took his license without a word & examined it & looked over the new Harley. "I've had a tough shift & this is my last pull over. I don't feel like more paperwork so if you can give me an excuse for your speeding that I haven't heard before I will let you go!"

"Last week my old lady ran off with a cop," the biker said, "and I was afraid you were trying to give her back!"

"Have a nice night", said the officer.

WATER IN THE CARBURETOR

Biker Joe's Old Lady comes home & tells her husband, "Dear, something is wrong with my bike. I know it has got to be water in the carburetor."

Biker Joe replies, "There is no way that is possible."

"Well," says his wife, "I'm telling you that's the problem."

Biker Joe gets up & sighs, "OK, fine. Where'd you park it?"

His Old Lady points toward the backyard, "In the swimming pool."

YUPPIE BIKER RUNS STOP SIGN

A police officer had just pulled over a yuppie on a new Harley for running a stop sign. "May I see your driver's license & registration please?" the officer asked.

"What's the problem, officer?" the yuppie replied.

"You just ran a stop sign." the officer said.

"Oh, come on, pal, there wasn't a single car anywhere in sight."

"Nevertheless sir, you are required to come to a complete stop, look both ways, & only then proceed with caution."

"You've got to be kidding me!" the yuppie said.

"It's no joke sir." the officer said, pulling out his book & preparing to write a ticket.

"Look I slowed down almost to a complete stop, saw no one, & proceeded with caution!"

The officer sighed & slowly shook his head. "Sir, you're supposed to come to a complete stop & you didn't. Now, may I see your license & registration?"

"You sure do have a lot of time on your hands pal. What's the matter, all the doughnut shops closed this early?" the yuppie asked sneering.

"SIR!" The officer sighed. "I'll over look that last comment now let me see your license & registration immediately!"

"I will, if you can tell me the difference between slowing down, & coming to a complete stop." the yuppie said, folding his arms across his chest.

A smile appeared on the officer's face. "Sir, I can do better than that." The police officer quickly jerked the rude guy off his Harley, & proceeded to methodically beat him over the head with his nightstick. "Now sir, would you like for me to slow down or come to a complete stop?"

THE FASTEST MOTORCYCLE

A man goes out & buys the best & most expensive motorcycle available, a 2019 Turbo BeepBeep. He takes it out for a spin & while doing so, stops at red light. An old man on a moped pulls up by him. The old man looks over the sleek, shiny surface of the motorcycle & asks "What kind of motorcycle ya got there, sonny?"

The dude replies "A 2019 Turbo BeepBeep that costs $3,500,000."

"That's a lotta money! Why is it so expensive?" asks the old man.

"Cause this bike run 320 MPH!" states the cool dude proudly.

The old man asks "Can I sit on it?"

"Sure" replies the owner.

So, the old man saddles up & looks at all the gauges in awe. He gets back on his moped & says "That's a pretty nice motorcycle, alright!"

Just then the light changes, so the guy decides to show the old man what his motorcycle can do. He floors it, & within 30 seconds the speedometer reads 320 mph. Suddenly, the guy notices a dot in his rear-view mirror. It seems to be getting closer!

Whhoooooooooooosshhh! Something whips by him! Going maybe twice as fast! The guy wonders "What on earth could be going faster than my Turbo BeepBeep?" Then, ahead of him, he sees a dot coming toward him. Whoooooooooosh! Goes by again! And, it almost looked like the old man on the moped! Couldn't be thinks the guy. How could a moped outrun a Turbo BeepBeep? Again, he sees a dot in his rearview mirror! Whhoooooooooooosshhh-BLAM! It plows into the back of his bike.

The guy jumps off & discovers it is the old man! The guy runs up to the dying old man & asks "You're hurt bad! Is there anything I can do for you?"

Old man replies "Yeah, unhook my suspenders from your mirror.

A BRIDGE TO HAWAII

While riding along a California beach, a biker saw the sky split suddenly & then heard the booming voice of God say "Since you have been faithful to me in all ways, I will grant you one wish."

The biker pondered this awhile & then said, "Lord, I would like a bridge to Hawaii so I can go there anytime I want."

The Lord said "Can't you think of a request that would honor & glorify my name."

The biker thought about it & finally said, "Lord, I wish I could understand my wife. Please give me the ability to know how she feels, what she's thinking when she gives me the silent treatment, why she cries, what her hopes & dreams are, what she really means when she says nothing is wrong & how I can make her truly happy!"

God pauses & then replies "How many lanes do you want on that bridge to Hawaii?"

DOBERMAN VS POODLE PUPPY

A highly timid little man, ventured into a biker bar in the Bronx & clearing his throat asked, "Um, err, which of you gentlemen owns the Doberman tied outside to the parking meter?"

A giant of a man, wearing biker leathers, his body hair growing out through the seams, turned slowly on his stool, looked down at the quivering little man & said, "It's my dog. Why?"

"Well," squeaked the little man, obviously very nervous, "I believe my dog just killed it, sir."

"What?" roared the big man in disbelief. "What in the heck kinda of dog do you have?"

"Sir," answered the little man, "It's a four-week-old poodle puppy."

"Bull!" roared the biker, "How could your poodle puppy kill my Doberman?"

"It appears that your Doberman tried to swallow it whole & choked on my poodle puppy, sir."

BIKER & MEXICAN BORDER

A biker tries to cross the Mexican border on a motorcycle with two big bags strapped down to his rear fender. The border guard asks, "What's in the bags?" Biker says, "Sand!" The guard wants to examine them, so the motorcyclist gets off his scoot, places the bags on the ground, opens them up, & the guard inspects... only to find sand. The biker straps the bags of sand back onto his scoot & goes on across the border.

Two weeks later, the same situation is repeated... "What have you there?" "Sand" "We want to examine." Same results... nothing but sand & he is on his way again.

Every two weeks for six months the inspections continue. Finally, one week the old biker didn't show up. However, the guard sees him downtown & says to him, "Buddy, you had us crazy. We sorta knew you were smuggling something. I won't say anything, but what were you smuggling?"

The biker says, "Motorcycles."

BE QUIET PASSING ROOM #7

A biker arrives at the gates of heaven. St. Peter asks, "Denomination?"

The biker says, "Methodist."

St. Pete looks down his list, & says, "Go to room 21, but be very quiet passing room 7."

Another biker arrives at the gates of heaven. "Denomination?"

"Lutheran."

"Go to room 14, but be very quiet as you pass room 7."

A third biker arrives at the gates. "Denomination?"

"Presbyterian."

"Go to room 17, but be very quiet as you pass room 7."

The biker says, "I can understand there being different rooms for different denominations, but why must I be quiet when I pass room 7?"

St. Peter tells him, "Well the Baptists are in room 7, & they think they're the only ones here.

ATHEIST & LOCH NESS MONSTER

Biker George heard this story about an atheist was rowing on Loch Ness in Scotland.

One day, all of a sudden, the Loch Ness monster attacked & grabbed him from his boat.

He panicked & shouted "God help me!" & suddenly, the monster & everything around him just froze.

A voice from the heavens boomed "You say you don't believe in me, but now you're asking for my help?"

The atheist looked up & said, "Well, ten seconds ago I didn't believe in the Loch Ness Monster either."

PRAY FOR BUBBA'S HEARING

Bubba wasn't his happy self when he came to church on Sunday. After church he didn't leave right away as he usually does either. Instead, he bowed his head & put his head in his hands like something wasn't well.

"What's wrong, Bubba?" asked the pastor.

"I need you to pray for my hearing," said Bubba.

The pastor laid hands on Bubba's ears & prayed for several minutes.

When he was done, he asked, "So how's your hearing?"

"I don't know," said Bubba. "It isn't until next Tuesday."

JESUS IS GONNA GET YOU

A thief broke into a Christian Biker's house late at night when he heard a voice say "Jesus is gonna get you."

The robber ignores it, grabs some more valuables, then he hears it again… "Jesus is gonna get you."

The robber starts to get a little worried & then notices it's just a parrot & says "What's your name, birdie?" "Moses." "What idiot would name you Moses?"

"The same idiot who calls his rottweiler Jesus."

ANYONE KNOW HOW TO PRAY?

A Christian Biker takes one of those cruise ships to the Bahamas.

There was this real bad storm raging when the captain realized his ship was sinking fast.

The Captain gave a desperate shout out, "Anyone here know how to pray?"

The Christian Biker stepped forward. "Aye, Captain, I know how to pray."

"Good," said the captain, "you pray while the rest of us put on our life jackets... we're one short."

MEAN DOG & LITTLE UGLY DOG

There was a big tough biker who owned a big tough Great Dane. Now this Great Dane was a very mean dog… definitely not the kind of dog you want jumping up in your lap.

One day, as the biker was walking his Great Dane, he saw a guy walking a little bitty dog with short legs no tail & no hair. It was an ugly dog, & frankly it looked sick.

Suddenly the Great Dane saw the little ugly dog across the street & decided he hated that dog. He broke free from his owner's leash & dashed across the street on the attack. The owner of the Great Dane yelled at the man, "Look out! My dog is on the loose & he is liable to kill you & that dog of yours! You had better run!"

The little ugly dog just looked up at the viscous dog as it was almost on top of him. Then the little dog proceeded to grab hold of the Great Dane at the foreleg & began to eat that big dog up. It ate right up the leg, right up the throat, ate its head, right down through the body, right across the tail, right down the back legs, spit out the bones, & smacked its lips… & that was the end of the mean Great Dane, just like that.

Well, the owner of the Great Dane was absolutely astonished by what he had just witnessed. "Man, what kind of dog is that?" the man exclaimed. "I've never in my life seen a little dog that could do something like that!"

"What Dog?" the other man said. "Before he got his nose & tail ran over by a big truck this was an alligator!"

BIKER DRANK BRAKE FLUID

While working on a motorcycle, a mechanic accidentally swallowed some brake fluid & he actually liked the taste.

The next day he decided to have another swig & enjoyed it so much that he told his friend.

His friend said: "You shouldn't be drinking brake fluid. It's bad for you."

But the mechanic was hooked, & drinking some every day. His friend was really worried about him.

"You've got to give it up," he insisted. "Brake fluid is poisonous."

"Don't worry," said the mechanic. "I can stop anytime."

BIKER CHICK MOPPED FLOOR

A police officer responds to a shots fired call & jumps into his squad car with blue lights & sirens blaring.

He gets to the house & is briefed on the situation.

He then calls the station & tells them, "I have an interesting case here."

"This biker chick shot her old man for stepping on the floor she just mopped."

"Have you arrested her?" asks the sergeant.

"No, not yet. The floor's still wet."

BAPTIZED IN CHURCH POND

What a glorious day it was when Biker Bob & his old lady had Little Johnny baptized in the church pond.

However, Little Johnny cried all the way home in the back seat of their truck.

Bob kept asking him what was wrong.

Finally, Johnny replied... "That pastor said that he was looking forward to seeing me being brought up in a good Christian home!

But I really want to stay with y'all!"

BIKER GEORGE PASSES GAS

Biker George was in a restaurant full of people all over the place, when he desperately needed to pass gas.

He couldn't hold it in any longer, & since the music was really loud, he timed his reliefs to the beat of the music.

After a couple songs, he started to feel better.

George finished his drink, & noticed that everybody was staring at him...

That was when he remembered he was listening to his iPod.

BIKER PAINTS TO EARN GAS MONEY

An old scruffy biker runs out of gas in front of a beautiful mansion with a shiny new Cadillac parked on the side. He knocks on the big door & asks the lady who owns the house if she could spare a few bucks for gas.

The woman thinks to herself for a few seconds, then says, "If you paint my porch for me, I'd be glad to give you $20. There's some green paint & a brush around the corner over there, have at it."

He thanks her, & heads for the paint & brush.

After about an hour, she gets up to check on his progress, & she sees that he hasn't even started on the porch yet.

Just then, she hears a knocking again at her door, & goes to open it. She is greeted by the old biker with green paint splattered on his clothes & in his beard, a wide grin on his face. "All done mam, & by the way, it's a Caddy, not a Porsche."

FATHER CAUGHT SPEEDING

Father O'Malley was riding his Harley on Christmas Eve when got stopped for speeding. The cop smelled alcohol on the priest's breath & then saw an empty wine bottle sticking out of a saddle bag.

The officer said, 'Father, have you been drinking?'

'Only water', replied Father O'Malley.

The cop asked, 'Then how come I can smell wine?'

The priest looked at the bottle & said, 'Good Lord! He's done it again!'

TELL A DUMB BLONDE JOKE?

Biker George is at a rally & asks a biker chick sitting next to him if she wants to hear a dumb blonde joke.

The biker chick replies "Well, before you tell me that joke, you should know something. I'm blonde, six feet tall, 240 lbs. & I'm a professional boxer.

Also, the blonde woman sitting next to me is 6'2", weighs 245 lbs. & is a professional wrestler.

Next to her is a blonde who is 6'5", weighs 250 lbs. & she's a world champion kickboxer.

Now, do you still want to tell me that blonde joke?"

George thinks about it a second & says: "Nah, not if I'm gonna have to explain it three times."

BIKER GEORGE & HORSE RIDING

Biker George had a near-death experience which changed his life forever.

This life changing event came about when he decided to go horseback riding one day.

Everything was going fine until the horse started bouncing out of control.

George tried with all his might to hang on, but was thrown off & his foot became caught in the stirrup. When this happened, he landed head-first to the ground. His head continued to bounce harder as the horse would not stop or even slow down.

Just as he was giving up hope & losing consciousness... a thoughtful K-Mart manager came out & pulled the plug.

LITTLE GUY & THE BIG BIKER

A little guy gets on a plane & sits next to the window. A few minutes later, a big heavily tattooed biker plops down in the seat next to him & immediately falls asleep.

The little guy starts to feel a little airsick, but he's afraid to wake the big biker up to ask if he can go to the bathroom. He knows he can't climb over him, & so the little guy is sitting there, looking at the big biker, trying to decide what to do.

Suddenly, the plane hits an air pocket & an uncontrollable wave of nausea passes through the little guy. He can't hold it in any longer & he pukes all over the biker's chest.

About five minutes later the big biker wakes up, looks down, & sees the vomit all over him. "So," says the little guy, "are you feeling better now?"

TEXAS BIKER & GREAT BEYOND

A biker from Texas died & went to the Great Beyond.

As he approached the great gate, he didn't see the streets of gold off in the distance but noticed that the terrain was bare with no greenery.

He saw the gate keeper & said "Howdy Saint Pete... this looks sorta like where I come from in Texas." I appreciate you fixing this place up to be like my homeplace in Texas! I'm sure I'll feel right at home here."

"The gatekeeper replied, "First of all, I'm not Saint Pete & second, you really don't know where you are, do you?

LOT'S WIFE TURNED INTO SALT

The Sunday School teacher was talking about back in the book of Genesis when Lot & his family were fleeing from Sodom.

As they made their escape, one angel commanded Lot not to look back.

However, as Sodom & Gomorrah were destroyed with brimstone & fire from the Lord, Lot's wife looked back at the city of Sodom & she turned into a pillar of salt.

A biker's young child interrupted & said, "My mommy looked back once while she was riding & she turned into a telephone pole."

CHILD SAVED FROM MEAN DOG

A biker is riding through a small town when he hears the screams of a little girl being attacked by a vicious dog. He jumps off his motorcycle & wrestles the savage mongrel but ends up having to break its neck in order to save the girl's life.

A reporter for the local newspaper who saw part of the action scene walks over & says: You're a hero! Tomorrow it will be in all the newspapers. Brave soldier saves the life of little girl!

Biker replies: But I am not a soldier! Reporter says: I saw your helmet, so what are you then?

Biker replies: It's a motorcycle helmet! I'm a motorcyclist!

The next day... Headlines read: Crazed Biker Kills Cute Little Doggy!

LITTLE LIP PRINTS ON MIRROR

Biker George worked at a private school as a part-time janitor a long time ago.

There was a certain problem there when some of the 12-year-old girls were starting to use lipstick. They'd put it on in the bathroom & then press their lips to the mirror, leaving a bunch of little lip prints. Every night he'd remove them, but they would reappear the next day.

Finally, the principal decided to end this problem & asked Biker George to show the girls how hard it was to clean these mirrors.

George took out a long-handled squeegee, dipped it in the toilet, & cleaned the mirrors with it. Since that day they have not had any problems with lip prints on any of those mirrors!

BIKER & THE TALKING FROG

An old biker found a frog sitting next to him in a park.

He noticed the frog was looking at him, when it suddenly said, "Kiss me & I will become a beautiful princess."

The biker was in shock as he studied the frog. Then he grabbed it up & put it in his pocket.

A little while later he decided to check on the little froggy, & asked "Is everything OK down there in my pocket?"

"Well, not really" the frog croaked, "I need you to kiss me so I can become a beautiful princess & we can get married & live happily ever after."

The biker says, "I'll talk to you later" & closes up his pocket.

About an hour later he hears the frog trying to talk to him from his pocket. He opens his pocket & asks the frog "What's up?"

The frog asks him "How come you didn't kiss me?"

Biker replies, "I'd rather have a talking frog that's worth more than a princess any day!"

BIKER TEACHES SELF-ESTEEM

Biker George was asked if he'd be the guest teacher at school for a day.

He thought it would be a great opportunity to teach students about self-esteem.

He said to the class "Everyone who thinks you are dumb, please stand up."

He didn't think anybody would stand, & was gonna make a point how nobody really is dumb, but about that same time one little kid stood up.

He didn't quite know what to do. So, he asked "Do you really think you're dumb?"

The kid said "No Sir, I just hate to see you standing there all by yourself."

A MERRY HEART DOES GOOD LIKE A MEDICINE

BIKER NIGHT B4 CHRISTMAS

Twas the night before Christmas, & all through the pad,
There was nada happenin', now that's pretty sad.
The woodstove was hung up in that stocking routine,
In hopes that the Fat Boy would soon make the scene.
With our stomachs full of hot chocolate cheer,
Wearing Harley jamas & new footy gear.
When out in the yard there arose such a racket,
I ran for the door & grabbed me my jacket.
I saw a large bro' on a '56 Pan,
Wearin' leathers & boots, a cool biker, man.
Strapped to the bike was a bikeful of sacks,
And that Pan hit the roof like running on tracks.
I couldn't help gawking, he flew like a deer.
But I had to go in… I was freezing my rear.
Down through the stovepipe he fell with a crash,
And out of the stove he came dragging his stash.
With a grin & some glee he passed out the loot,
A new jacket for her & some chrome for my scoot.
He gave us a smile & then a high five,
Spun on his heel then up he did ride.
From up on the roof came a great deal of thunder,
As that massive V-twin ripped the silence asunder.
With beard in the wind, he roared off in the night,
Shouting, "Have a cool Yule, & to all a good ride!"

Merry Heart Scriptures

Genesis 21:6 (KJV) & Sarah said, God hath made me to laugh, so that all that hear will laugh with me.

Job 8:21 (KJV) Till he fill thy mouth with laughing, & thy lips with rejoicing.

Psalms 2:4 (KJV) He that sitteth in the heavens shall laugh: the Lord shall have them in derision.

Psalms 16:11 (KJV) Thou wilt shew me the path of life: in thy presence is fulness of joy; at thy right hand there are pleasures for evermore.

Psalms 32:11 (KJV) Be glad in the LORD, & rejoice, ye righteous: & shout for joy, all ye that are upright in heart.

Psalms 37:4 (KJV) Delight thyself also in the LORD; & he shall give thee the desires of thine heart.

Psalms 126:2 (KJV) Then was our mouth filled with laughter, & our tongue with singing: then said they among the heathen, The LORD hath done great things for them.

Proverbs 3:13-18 (KJV) Happy is the man that findeth wisdom, & the man that getteth understanding. For the merchandise of it is better than the merchandise of silver, & the gain thereof than fine gold. She is more precious than rubies: & all the things thou canst desire are not to be compared unto her. Length of days is in her right hand; & in her left hand riches & honour. Her ways are ways of pleasantness, & all her paths are peace. She is a tree of life to them that lay hold upon her: & happy is every one that retaineth her.

Proverbs 15:13 (KJV) A merry heart maketh a cheerful countenance: but by sorrow of the heart the spirit is broken.

Proverbs 17:22 (KJV) A merry heart doeth good like a medicine: but a broken spirit drieth the bones.

Ecclesiastes 3:4 (KJV) A time to weep, & a time to laugh; a time to mourn, & a time to dance;

Ecclesiastes 3:12 (KJV) I know that there is no good in them, but for a man to rejoice, & to do good in his life.

Ecclesiastes 3:13 (KJV) & also that every man should eat & drink, & enjoy the good of all his labour, it is the gift of God.

Isaiah 12:3 (KJV) Therefore with joy shall ye draw water out of the wells of salvation.

John 16:22 (KJV) & ye now therefore have sorrow: but I will see you again, & your heart shall rejoice, & your joy no man taketh from you.

John 16:24 (KJV) Hither to have ye asked nothing in my name: ask, & ye shall receive, that your joy may be full.

Romans 12:12 (KJV) Rejoicing in hope; patient in tribulation; continuing instant in prayer;

Romans 14:17 (KJV) For the kingdom of God is not meat & drink; but righteousness, & peace, & joy in the Holy Ghost.

Romans 15:13 (KJV) Now the God of hope fill you with all joy & peace in believing, that ye may abound in hope, through the power of the Holy Ghost.

2 Corinthians 12:10 (KJV) Therefore I take pleasure in infirmities, in reproaches, in necessities, in persecutions, in distresses for Christ's sake: for when I am weak, then am I strong.

Galatians 5:22 (KJV) But the fruit of the Spirit is love, joy, peace, longsuffering, gentleness, goodness, faith,

Philippians 4:4 (KJV) Rejoice in the Lord alway: & again I say, Rejoice.

Philippians 4:7 (KJV) & the peace of God, which passeth all understanding, shall keep your hearts & minds through Christ Jesus.

1 Thessalonians 5:16 (KJV) Rejoice evermore.

1 Peter 1:8 (KJV) Whom having not seen, ye love; in whom, though now ye see him not, yet believing, ye rejoice with joy unspeakable & full of glory:

1 Peter 3:14 (KJV) But & if ye suffer for righteousness' sake, happy are ye: & be not afraid of their terror, neither be troubled;

Healing Scriptures

Exodus 15:26 (KJV) If thou wilt diligently hearken to the voice of the Lord thy God, & wilt do that which is right in his sight, & wilt give ear to his commandments, & keep all his statutes, I will put none of these diseases upon thee, which I have brought upon the Egyptians: for I am the Lord that healeth thee.

Exodus 23:25-26 (KJV) & ye shall serve the Lord your God, & he shall bless thy bread, & thy water; & I will take sickness away from the midst of thee. There shall nothing cast their young, nor be barren, in thy land: the number of thy days I will fulfill.

Deuteronomy 7:14-15 (KJV) Thou shalt be blessed above all people: there shall not be male or female barren among you, or among your cattle. & the Lord will take away from thee all sickness, & will put none of the evil diseases of Egypt, which thou knowest, upon thee; but will lay them upon all them that hate thee.

Deuteronomy 30:19-20 (KJV) I call heaven & earth to record this day against you, that I have set before you life & death, blessing & cursing: therefore choose life, that both thou & thy seed may live: That thou mayest love the Lord thy God, & that thou mayest obey his voice, & that thou mayest cleave unto him: for he is thy life, & the length of thy days: that thou mayest dwell in the land which the Lord sware unto thy fathers, to Abraham, to Isaac, & to Jacob, to give them.

1 Kings 8:56 (KJV) Blessed be the Lord, that hath given rest unto his people Israel, according to all that he promised: there hath not failed one word of all his good promise, which he promised by the hand of Moses his servant.

Psalm 91:9-10, 14-16 (KJV) Because thou hast made the Lord, which is my refuge, even the most High, thy habitation; there shall no evil befall thee, neither shall any plague come nigh thy dwelling. Because he hath set his love upon me, therefore will I deliver him: I will set him on high, because he hath known my name. He shall call upon me, & I will answer him: I will be with him in trouble; I will deliver him, & honour him. With long life will I satisfy him, & show him my salvation.

Psalm 103:1-5 (KJV) Bless the Lord, O my soul: & all that is within me, bless his holy name. Bless the Lord, O my soul, & forget not all his benefits: who forgiveth all thine iniquities; who healeth all thy diseases; who redeemeth thy life from destruction; who crowneth thee with lovingkindness & tender mercies; who satisfieth thy mouth with good things; so that thy youth is renewed like the eagle's.

Psalm 107:17, 19-21 (KJV) Fools because of their transgression, & because of their iniquities, are afflicted. Then they cry unto the Lord in their trouble, & he saveth them out of their distresses. He sent his word, & healed them, & delivered them from their destructions. Oh that men would praise the Lord for his goodness, & for his wonderful works to the children of men!

Psalm 118:17 (KJV) I shall not die, but live, & declare the works of the Lord.

Proverbs 4:20-24 (KJV) My son, attend to my words; incline thine ear unto my sayings. Let them not depart from thine eyes; keep them in the midst of thine heart. For they are life unto those that find them, & health to all their flesh. Keep thy heart with all diligence; for out of it are the issues of life. Put away from thee a froward mouth, & perverse lips put far from thee.

Isaiah 41:10 (KJV) Fear thou not; for I am with thee: be not dismayed; for I am thy God: I will strengthen thee; yea, I will help thee; yea, I will uphold thee with the right hand of my righteousness.

Isaiah 53:4-5 (KJV) Surely he hath borne our griefs, & carried our sorrows: yet we did esteem him stricken, smitten of God, & afflicted. But he was wounded for our transgressions, he was bruised for our iniquities: the chastisement of our peace was upon him; & with his stripes we are healed.

Jeremiah 1:12 (KJV) Then said the Lord unto me, Thou hast well seen: for I will hasten my word to perform it.

Jeremiah 17:14 (KJV) Heal me, O Lord, & I shall be healed; save me, & I shall be saved: for thou art my praise.

Jeremiah 30:17 (KJV) For I will restore health unto thee, & I will heal thee of thy wounds, saith the Lord.

Joel 3:10 (KJV) Beat your ploughshares into swords, & your pruning hooks into spears: let the weak say, I am strong.

Nahum 1:9 (KJV) What do ye imagine against the Lord? he will make an utter end: affliction shall not rise up the second time.

Matthew 8:2-3 (KJV) And, behold, there came a leper & worshipped him, saying, Lord, if thou wilt, thou canst make me clean. & Jesus put forth his hand, & touched him, saying, I will; be thou clean. & immediately his leprosy was cleansed.

Matthew 8:16-17 (KJV) When the even was come, they brought unto him many that were possessed with devils: & he cast out the spirits with his word, & healed all that were sick: that it might be fulfilled which was spoken by Esaias the prophet, saying, Himself took our infirmities, & bare our sicknesses.

Matthew 15:30-31 (KJV) & great multitudes came unto him, having with them those that were lame, blind, dumb, maimed, & many others, & cast them down at Jesus' feet; & he healed them: insomuch that the multitude wondered, when they saw the dumb to speak, the maimed to be whole, the lame to walk, & the blind to see: & they glorified the God of Israel.

Matthew 18:18-19 (KJV) Verily I say unto you, Whatsoever ye shall bind on earth shall be bound in heaven: & whatsoever ye shall loose on earth shall be loosed in heaven. Again I say unto you, That if two of you shall agree on earth as touching any thing that they shall ask, it shall be done for them of my Father which is in heaven.

Matthew 21:21-22 (KJV) Jesus answered & said unto them, Verily I say unto you, If ye have faith, & doubt not, ye shall not only do this which is done to the fig tree, but also if ye shall say unto this mountain, Be thou removed, & be thou cast into the sea; it shall be done. & all things, whatsoever ye shall ask in prayer, believing, ye shall receive.

Mark 9:23 (KJV) Jesus said unto him, If thou canst believe, all things are possible to him that believeth.

Mark 10:27 (KJV) & Jesus looking upon them saith, With men it is impossible, but not with God: for with God all things are possible.

Mark 11:22-24 (KJV) & Jesus answering saith unto them, Have faith in God. For verily I say unto you, That whosoever shall say unto this mountain, Be thou removed, & be thou cast into the sea; & shall not doubt in his heart, but shall believe that those things which he saith shall come to pass; he shall have whatsoever he saith. Therefore I say unto you, What things soever ye desire, when ye pray, believe that ye receive them, & ye shall have them.

Mark 16:14-18 (KJV) Afterward he appeared unto the eleven as they sat at meat, & upbraided them with their unbelief & hardness of heart, because they believed not them which had seen him after he was risen. & he said unto them, Go ye into all the world, & preach the gospel to every creature. He that believeth & is baptized shall be saved; but he that believeth not shall be damned. & these signs shall follow them that believe; In my name shall they cast out devils; they shall speak with new tongues; they shall take up serpents; & if they drink any deadly thing, it shall not hurt them; they shall lay hands on the sick, & they shall recover.

Luke 6:19 (KJV) & the whole multitude sought to touch him: for there went virtue out of him, & healed them all.

Luke 9:2 (KJV) & he sent them to preach the kingdom of God, & to heal the sick.

Luke 13:16 (KJV) & ought not this woman, being a daughter of Abraham, whom Satan hath bound, lo, these eighteen years, be loosed from this bond on the sabbath day?

Acts 5:16 (KJV) There came also a multitude out of the cities round about unto Jerusalem, bringing sick folks, & them which were vexed with unclean spirits: & they were healed every one.

Acts 10:38 (KJV) How God anointed Jesus of Nazareth with the Holy Ghost & with power: who went about doing good, & healing all that were oppressed of the devil; for God was with him.

Romans 4:16-21 (KJV) Therefore it is of faith, that it might be by grace; to the end the promise might be sure to all the seed; not to that only which is of the law, but to that also which is of the faith of Abraham; who is the father of us all, (as it is written, I have made thee a father of many nations,) before him whom he believed, even God, who quickeneth the dead, & calleth those things which be not as though they were. Who against hope believed in hope, that he might become the father of many nations, according to that which was spoken, So shall thy seed be. & being not weak in faith, he considered not his own body now dead, when he was about an hundred years old, neither yet the deadness of Sarah's womb: He staggered not at the promise of God through unbelief; but was strong in faith, giving glory to God; & being fully persuaded that, what he had promised, he was able also to perform.

Romans 8:2, 11 (KJV) For the law of the Spirit of life in Christ Jesus hath made me free from the law of sin & death. But if the Spirit of him that raised up Jesus from the dead dwell in you, he that raised up Christ from the dead shall also quicken your mortal bodies by his Spirit that dwelleth in you.

2 Corinthians 4:18 (KJV) While we look not at the things which are seen, but at the things which are not seen: for the things which are seen are temporal; but the things which are not seen are eternal.

2 Corinthians 10:3-5 (KJV) For though we walk in the flesh, we do not war after the flesh: (For the weapons of our warfare are not carnal, but mighty through God to the pulling down of strong holds;) casting down imaginations, & every high thing that exalteth itself against the knowledge of God, & bringing into captivity every thought to the obedience of Christ.

Galatians 3:13-14, 29 (KJV) Christ hath redeemed us from the curse of the law, being made a curse for us: for it is written, Cursed is every one that hangeth on a tree: that the blessing of Abraham might come on the Gentiles through Jesus Christ; that we might receive the promise of the Spirit through faith. & if ye be Christ's, then are ye Abraham's seed, & heirs according to the promise.

Ephesians 6:10-17 (KJV) Finally, my brethren, be strong in the Lord, & in the power of his might. Put on the whole armour of God, that ye may be able to stand against the wiles of the devil. For we wrestle not against flesh & blood, but against principalities, against powers, against the rulers of the darkness of this world, against spiritual wickedness in high places. Wherefore take unto you the whole armour of God, that ye may be able to withstand in the evil day, & having done all, to stand. Stand therefore, having your loins girt about with truth, & having on the breastplate of righteousness; & your feet shod with the preparation of the gospel of peace; above all, taking the shield of faith, wherewith ye shall be able to quench all the fiery darts of the wicked. & take the helmet of salvation, & the sword of the Spirit, which is the word of God.

Philippians 2:13 (KJV) For it is God which worketh in you both to will & to do of his good pleasure.

Philippians 4:6-9 (KJV) Be careful for nothing; but in every thing by prayer & supplication with thanksgiving let your requests be made known unto God. & the peace of God, which passeth all understanding, shall keep your hearts & minds through Christ Jesus. Finally, brethren, whatsoever things are true, whatsoever things are honest, whatsoever things are just, whatsoever things are pure, whatsoever things are lovely, whatsoever things are of good report; if there be any virtue, & if there be any praise, think on these things. Those things, which ye have both learned, & received, & heard, & seen in me, do: & the God of peace shall be with you.

2 Timothy 1:7 (KJV) For God hath not given us the spirit of fear; but of power, & of love, & of a sound mind.

Hebrews 10:23 (KJV) Let us hold fast the profession of our faith without wavering; (for he is faithful that promised).

Hebrews 10:35-36 (KJV) Cast not away therefore your confidence, which hath great recompence of reward. For ye have need of patience, that, after ye have done the will of God, ye might receive the promise.

Hebrews 11:11 (KJV) Through faith also Sarah herself received strength to conceive seed, & was delivered of a child when she was past age, because she judged him faithful who had promised.

Hebrews 13:8 (KJV) Jesus Christ the same yesterday, & today, & for ever.

James 4:7 (KJV) Submit yourselves therefore to God. Resist the devil, & he will flee from you.

James 5:14-16 (KJV) Is any sick among you? let him call for the elders of the church; & let them pray over him, anointing him with oil in the name of the Lord: & the prayer of faith shall save the sick, & the Lord shall raise him up; & if he have committed sins, they shall be forgiven him. Confess your faults one to another, & pray one for another, that ye may be healed. The effectual fervent prayer of a righteous man availeth much.

1 Peter 2:24 (KJV) Who his own self bare our sins in his own body on the tree, that we, being dead to sins, should live unto righteousness: by whose stripes ye were healed.

1 John 3:21-22 (KJV) Beloved, if our heart condemn us not, then have we confidence toward God. & whatsoever we ask, we receive of him, because we keep his commandments, & do those things that are pleasing in his sight.

1 John 5:14-15 (KJV) & this is the confidence that we have in him, that, if we ask any thing according to his will, he heareth us: & if we know that he hear us, whatsoever we ask, we know that we have the petitions that we desired of him.

A MERRY HEART DOES GOOD LIKE A MEDICINE

EPILOGUE

The starting point for any relationship with God is accepting the free gift of salvation through Jesus Christ. You can't ride with Him & be in God's Winner's Circle if you haven't accepted Him into your life & allowed Him to become your Lord & Savior. Romans 10:9 (NLT) says If you openly declare that Jesus is Lord & believe in your heart that God raised him from the dead, you will be saved. GOD LOVES YOU & WILL GIVE YOU A MERRY HEART WITH PEACE & ETERNITY IN HEAVEN THROUGH HIS SON JESUS.

★ WHAT YOU MUST DO:

1. Admit your need (I am a sinner). 2. Be willing to turn from sin (repent). 3. Believe Jesus died for you (On the Cross) & rose from the dead. 4. Through prayer (Talking to God) invite Jesus Christ to come in & control your life. (Receive Him as Savior & Lord).

★ WHAT TO PRAY:

Dear Father, I know that I am a sinner & need forgiveness. I believe that Christ died for my sin. I am willing to turn from sin. I now invite Jesus Christ to come into my heart & life as my personal savior. I am willing, by God's grace, to follow & obey Jesus Christ as the Lord of my life.

If you accepted Jesus as your Savior, then this is just the beginning of an awesome ride down the road of life with Jesus Christ.

★ NEXT STEPS:

1. Read your Bible every day to get to know Christ better.
2. Talk to God in prayer every day.
3. Tell others about Christ.
4. Be baptized, worship, fellowship & serve with other Christians in a church where the Bible is preached.
5. Let me know so I can rejoice with you!

About the Author

Dano lives in the south-central part of North Carolina with his beautiful wife T. Family life as a son, husband, brother, father, grandfather, & great grandfather are very important to him. Dano has also been an integral part of the motorcycle community for years & has traveled worldwide sharing the Gospel of our Lord Jesus Christ. As an author, his hope is that the Biker George Books will be like a fresh breeze from the Holy Spirit in a hot desert. The *Biker George Daily Ride Devotionals* were written to help inspire you to ride with the Lord Jesus Christ every day. The *Biker George Clean Humor + Biker Joke Books* were written to put a smile on your face & to give you a merry heart that can help with healing & good health! Biker George would like to encourage you to get into God's Word daily & to smile & laugh often!

Proverbs 17:22 (KJV) A merry heart doeth good like a medicine: but a broken spirit drieth the bones

The fact that I am a biker doesn't make me a different kinda Christian. But the fact that I'm a Christian does make me a different kinda biker.
Get more books by Dano: Amazon.com/author/dano
Keep up with Biker George: Facebook.com/BikerGeorgeBook

Special thanks to Rich @ Vreeland's Harley-Davidson for sponsoring Biker George Clean Humor + Biker Joke Book Vol.1.

VREELAND'S HARLEY-DAVIDSON
www.VreelandsHarley.com

317 Montour Blvd, Bloomsburg, PA 17815

(570) 784-2453

sales@vreelandsharley.com • service@vreelandsharley.com

A MERRY HEART DOES GOOD LIKE A MEDICINE

Vreeland Winner's Circle

ALL THE FOLLOWING BIKES WON WITH A VREELAND RACING ENGINE!!!

RICH VREELAND WINS AGAIN!
2018 AMRA NITRO FUNNY BIKE CHAMPIONSHIP
AT ROCKINGHAM, NC (THE ROCK)

RICH VREELAND WINS NATIONALS AGAIN!

ANDY HORN WINS IN MICHIGAN AMRA SUPER GAS AT US 131 DRAGWAY!

ANDY HORN WINS AT THE NUMIDIA AMRA SUPERGAS!

BRAD SMITH AT PMRA WORLD FINALS
WINS WITH THE RAY VREELAND RACING ENGINE!

RICH KOPEC WINS AT LEBANON VALLEY NY!

KIM KINIRY WINS AGAIN ON HIS 1550 CC STROKER V-ROD LEBANON VALLEY NY!

A MERRY HEART DOES GOOD LIKE A MEDICINE

RICH VREELAND & BILLY ROWE WIN AGAIN!

STEVE MATTHEWS GETS THE WALLY ON A VREELAND'S POWERED V-ROD AT NHRA ROUTE 66 NATIONALS!

LORENZO CAPOGNA WON THE MODIFIED BIKE CLASS
AT THE ATURA SIDNEY, AUSTRALIA EVENT
USING A VREELAND'S RACING PARTS STROKER KIT.
THE BIKE WAS RUNNING IN THE "8"S ALL WEEKEND!!!

A MERRY HEART DOES GOOD LIKE A MEDICINE

BILL ROWE, RAY, RICH, & PATTI VREELAND. BILL HAD AN OUTSTANDING SEASON. 8 NHRA WALLYS & 4 AMRA WINS WITH HIS VREELAND'S RACING BUILT DESTROYERS!

RAY VREELAND'S RACING ENGINES HAD A TRIPLE WIN AT AMRA MICHIGAN RACE. DENNIS WALDRON WON SUPER GAS & TOP ELIMINATOR BILLY ROWE WON SUPER PRO!

KIM KINIRY WINS AGAIN!!!
THANKS TO THE RAY VREELAND ENGINE!

KIM KINIRY WINS AT LEBANON VALLEY
WITH A RAY VREELAND ENGINE!

A MERRY HEART DOES GOOD LIKE A MEDICINE

BILL ROWE JR. WON SUPER PRO AT
THE AMRA CAJUN BLOWOUT IN BATON ROUGE
ON A RAY VREELAND PREPARED V-ROD!

KEVIN CLEMENTS WINS AHDRA!

RICH VREELAND AT ORLANDO ON HIS V-ROD!

RICH VREELAND'S SUPER GAS DESTROYER WINS!

WANDA POFF WINS WITH HER
VREELAND'S RACING BUILT DESTROYER!

DENNIS WALDRON AT NORWALK ON HIS DESTROYER!

DEREK CHRISTENSEN AT ROCKINGHAM, NC ON HIS V-ROD!

BILL ROWE AT BRISTOL ON HIS DESTROYER!

A MERRY HEART DOES GOOD LIKE A MEDICINE

JARAD BAKER
AT BOWLING GREEN, KY ON HIS V-ROD!

DAVID ISRAEL AT THE NORTHEAST NITRO NATIONALS
ON HIS 200 HP 1550 CC VREELAND'S BUILT V-ROD!

RICH VREELAND'S WIN AT BELLE ROSE, LA!

DENNIS WALDRON FROM BELLE ROSE, LA WON THE 2012 SUPER GAS CHAMPIONSHIP!

A MERRY HEART DOES GOOD LIKE A MEDICINE

Special thanks to Rich @ Vreeland's Harley-Davidson for sponsoring Biker George Clean Humor + Biker Joke Book Vol.1.

VREELAND'S HARLEY-DAVIDSON
www.VreelandsHarley.com

317 Montour Blvd, Bloomsburg, PA 17815

(570) 784-2453

sales@vreelandsharley.com • service@vreelandsharley.com

[notes]

Printed in Great Britain
by Amazon